THE
A MAN WALKS INTO A BAR...
JOKES

Billy Brownless

ALLEN&UNWIN

First published in 2009

Allen & Unwin
83 Alexander Street
Crows Nest NSW 2065
Australia
Phone: (61 2) 8425 0100
Fax: (61 2) 9906 2218
Email: info@allenandunwin.com
Web: www.allenandunwin.com

National Library of Australia
Cataloguing-in-Publication entry:

   Brownless, Anthony William, 1967-
   A man walks into a bar…: the best jokes / Billy Brownless.

   ISBN: 978 1 74237 156 6 (pbk.)

   Subjects: Bars (Drinking establishments)—Humour.
   Australian wit and humour.
   647.940207

Text design by Pauline Haas, Bluerinse Setting
Typesetting by Megan Ellis
Printed in Australia by McPherson's Printing Group
1 3 5 7 9 10 8 6 4 2

A MAN WALKS INTO A BAR...

Have a frothie on me
and enjoy the read!

Jokes that everyone has heard a thousand times already but they're (mostly) still funny

 Jokes about celebrities or well-known people

HUH? Jokes I don't get (but brainy people might)

CONTENTS

MAN'S BEST FRIEND

A MAN WALKS INTO A BAR with his little Jack Russell terrier. He puts the dog on the barstool next to his. The bartender wanders over and the man says, 'I'll have a pot thanks, mate.' The dog says, 'I'll have a margarita.'

The bartender does a double-take and looks over to the dog and asks, 'Did you just talk?'

'Yep,' says the dog.

'My God!' says the bartender. 'That's incredible. This is unreal. Who would have thought: a talking dog, here in my bar? Tell me more about yourself. You must have had an amazing life as a talking dog.'

The dog assumes an indifferent pose and speaks in quite a matter-of-fact manner:

'Yeah, you could say it's been a big journey. I trained for a while with the US Marines. Saw a bit of action in Iraq – can't tell you more. I joined the Bolshoi Ballet for a stint. That was hard work but incredibly satisfying. I've written a few best-selling novels in my spare time. That was good fun. Of course, there have been film offers, TV shows. Wine, women and song. All that.'

The bartender is now purple with excitement. He turns to the man. 'We could make a fortune. We could charge people to come into this bar and hear your dog talk. How much would you charge to allow your dog to talk here?'

'About $10,' the man replies.

'Why only $10? That's madness!' exclaims the bartender.

The man answers: 'He's a liar. He hasn't done half those things.'

A MAN WALKS INTO A BAR wearing dark glasses, accompanied by a chihuahua on a leash. The bartender says, 'Sorry, no dogs allowed.'

'I'm blind. It's my seeing-eye dog,' the man explains.

The bartender scoffs. 'Seeing-eye dogs are labradors or German shepherds.'

The man looks alarmed. 'What've they given me?'

A DOG WALKS INTO A BAR and says, 'Hey, bartender, can't a talking dog get a drink in here?'

'Yeah, dog,' says the bartender, 'the toilet's right around the corner there!'

A DOG HOBBLES INTO A BAR with his leg wrapped in bandages. He sidles up to the bartender and announces: 'I'm lookin' fer the man that shot my paw.'

A TOURIST WALKS INTO A BAR and there's a dog sitting in a chair, playing poker. The tourist says, 'Is that dog really playing poker?'

The bartender says, 'Yeah, but he's not too good. Whenever he has a good hand, he starts wagging his tail.'

HUH?

A BAR WALKS INTO A COMMUTATIVE algebraist.

A MAN WALKS INTO A BAR and sits down next to a lady and a dog. The man asks, 'Does your dog bite?'

The lady answers, 'Never!'

The man reaches out to pat the dog and the dog bites him. The man says, 'I thought you said your dog doesn't bite!'

The woman replies, 'He doesn't. This isn't my dog.'

A BLIND MAN WALKS INTO A BAR, grabs his dog, and starts swinging him around.

The bartender says, 'Hey mate, what are you doing?'

The blind man says, 'Don't mind me, I'm just looking around.'

A MAN WALKS INTO A BAR with his dog on a leash. The bartender says, 'Man, that's a weird dog. He's stumpy-legged, pink, and doesn't have a tail, but I bet my Rottweiler would beat the heck out of him.'

Fifty bucks is laid down. Out in the yard the Rottweiler gets mauled to pieces.

Another drinker says his pit bull will win. The bet is $100. There's another trip to the yard and when it's all over there are bits of pit bull terrier all over the place. The drinker pays up and says, 'So what breed is that anyway?'

The owner says, 'Until I cut his tail off and painted him pink he was the same breed as every other crocodile.'

A MAN WALKS INTO A BAR with his dog. He puts the dog on the bar and says to the bartender, 'This is the smartest dog in the world. I bet $5 that you can ask him anything and he will tell you the right answer.'

So the bartender says, 'All right. What is 10 + 11 + 13?'

The dog says, '34.'

'Wow,' says the bartender and hands over the $5 note.

Then the man says to the bartender, 'Don't let my dog go anywhere, I have to go to the toilet.'

He hands the dog the $5 to hold onto while he's in the toilet. The bartender and the dog start having a conversation and the bartender says, 'If you're so smart, go down the road and get me a newspaper.' So the dog leaves, and then the man comes out of the toilet. He asks the bartender where the dog is.

The bartender says, 'The dog went to get me a newspaper.'

The man throws a fit that the bartender let the dog leave. He goes out to find his dog. He looks all over until he sees his dog in an alley making love to a poodle. The man says, 'What are you doing? You've never done this before.'

The dog says, 'I've never had $5 before either.'

 **A SEAL WALKS INTO A CLUB ...**

A CHIHUAHUA, A DOBERMAN AND A BULLDOG WALK INTO A BAR for a drink. A great-looking female collie comes up to them and says, 'Whoever can say liver and cheese in a sentence can have me.'

So the Doberman says, 'I love liver and cheese.'

The collie replies, 'That's not good enough.'

The bulldog says, 'I hate liver and cheese.'

The collie says, 'That's not creative enough.'

Finally, the chihuahua says, 'Liver alone … cheese mine.'

HUH?

C, E-FLAT AND G GO INTO A BAR. The bartender says, 'Sorry, but we don't serve minors.'

DID YOU HEAR THE ONE ABOUT ...

A SAILOR AND A PIRATE WALK INTO A BAR. They sit down next to each other and get to talking. Their chat soon turns to their sea adventures. The sailor tells of his days fighting wars with the navy, and the pirate tells of robbing ships and killing his enemies. The sailor notices that the pirate has an eye patch, a hook and a peg leg, and asks, 'How did you get the peg leg?'

The pirate replies, 'When I was thrown off my ship and floated for two days until my crew rescued me, my leg was bitten off by a shark as I was being pulled out of the water.'

The sailor, impressed, says, 'Wow! That's very exciting. But what about the hook?'

The pirate smiles, shining the hook on his coat sleeve. 'When I was sword-fighting with an enemy pirate for treasure, he took it right off.'

The sailor's eyes are wide with awe at how tough this pirate is, and he asks, 'How did you get the eye patch?'

'Well,' says the pirate, shifting in his seat a bit, 'a seagull s*** in my eye.'

The sailor looks puzzled. 'You lost an eye from seagull s***?'

The pirate sighs and shakes his head. 'It was my first day with the hook.'

A MAGICIAN WALKS DOWN AN ALLEY and turns into a bar.

THE LONE RANGER AND TONTO WALK INTO A BAR in Texas on one of the hottest days on record and sit down to drink a beer. After a few minutes, a big tall cowboy walks in and says, 'Who owns the big white horse outside?'

The Lone Ranger stands up, hitches his gun belt, and says, 'I do ... why?'

The cowboy looks at the Lone Ranger and says, 'I just thought you'd like to know that your horse is just about dead from the heat.'

The Lone Ranger and Tonto rush outside and sure enough, Silver is ready to die from heat exhaustion. The Lone Ranger gets the horse some water and soon Silver is starting to feel a little better. The Lone Ranger turns to Tonto and says, 'Tonto, I want you to run around Silver and see if you can create enough of a breeze to make him feel better.'

Tonto says, 'Yes, Kemosabe,' and takes off running circles around Silver.

Not able to do anything but wait,
the Lone Ranger returns to the bar
to finish his drink. A few minutes
later, another cowboy struts into the
bar and asks, 'Who owns that big white
horse outside?'

The Lone Ranger stands again, and says,
'I do, what's wrong with him this time?'

The cowboy looks him in the eye and says …
'Nothing, but you left your Injun runnin'.'

CELINE DION WALKS INTO A BAR. The
bartender says, 'So, why the long face?'

A HEAD WALKS INTO A BAR and asks the bartender for a drink, and after he is finished, bang! a torso appears. So the head asks for another drink and after he finishes, bang! arms come out of the torso. So the head asks the bartender for another drink and when he has finished, bang! legs appear. The head is thinking, 'Hey, this stuff is great,' so he asks the bartender for one more drink for the road and bang! his whole body disappears.

The bartender turns to him and says, 'You should have quit while you were a head.'

A LEPRECHAUN WALKS INTO A BAR. The bartender serves him and says, 'That'll be $2.50.' The leprechaun puts two $1 coins on the bar and starts walking away.

The bartender shouts, 'You're a little short!'

A NEUTRON WALKS INTO A BAR and orders a drink. He asks the bartender, 'How much?'

'For you, sir, no charge.'

A SCRAWNY LITTLE MAN WALKS INTO A BAR, wearing thick glasses and a polyester suit. The bartender is the strongest man around and there is a long-standing $1000 bet among the patrons. The bartender will squeeze a lemon until all the juice runs into a glass, and hand the lemon to a patron. Anyone who can squeeze one more drop of juice out wins the money. Many people have tried over time but nobody can do it.

'I'd like to try the bet,' the little man says in a tiny, squeaky voice. After the laughter has died down, the bartender grabs a lemon and squeezes away. He hands the wrinkled remains of the rind to the little man. But the crowd's laughter turns to total silence as the man clenches his fist around the lemon and six drops fall into the glass. As the crowd cheers, the bartender pays the $1000 and asks the little man what he does for a living. Is he a lumberjack, or a weightlifter, or what?

'I work for the tax office.'

A SEWING MACHINE WALKS INTO A BAR, sits down, looks at the sewing machine sitting next to him and says, 'Do I know you, are you a singer?'

Sewing machine says, 'Ja-no-me?'

A NUMBER 12 WALKS INTO A BAR and asks the bartender for a pint of beer. 'Sorry, I can't serve you,' says the bartender.

'Why not?' asks the number 12 angrily.

'You're under 18,' replies the bartender.

A SOCCER BALL WALKS INTO A BAR.
The bartender kicks him out.

A BOOK WALKS INTO A BAR. The bartender
says, 'Please, no stories!'

A $5 NOTE WALKS INTO A BAR. The bartender
says, 'Get out! This is a singles bar.'

A GOLF CLUB WALKS INTO A BAR and orders a
beer, but the bartender refuses to serve him.

'Why not?' asks the golf club.

'You'll be driving later.'

A MAN WALKS INTO A BAR and orders a drink, then sits there looking at it for half an hour. Then a big trouble-making truck driver steps up next to the man, takes the drink from him and empties the glass. The poor man starts crying.

The truck driver says, 'Come on man, I was just joking. Here, I'll buy you another drink. I just can't stand seeing a man cry.'

'No, it's not that. This is the worst day of my life. First, I fall asleep and I'm late to my office. My boss, in an outrage, fires me. When I leave the building to get my car, I find out it's been stolen. The police say they can't do anything. I get a cab home and after I get out, I remember I left my wallet and credit cards inside. The cab driver just drives away. Inside, I find my wife sleeping with the gardener. I leave home and come to this bar. And when I was thinking about putting an end to my life, you show up and drink my poison.'

A COWBOY WALKS INTO A BAR. Upon leaving, he realises that someone has painted his horse. The cowboy yells, 'Which one of you painted my horse?'

A 7-foot-tall hulk of a man says, menacingly, 'I did.'

The cowboy realises he is in trouble and replies, 'Nice colour!'

A SKELETON WALKS INTO A BAR and says, 'Gimme a beer, and a mop.'

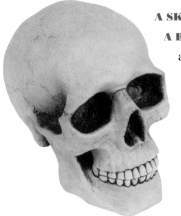

A MAN WALKS INTO A BAR and sees a friend at a table, drinking by himself. Approaching his friend, he comments, 'You look terrible. What's the matter?'

'My mother died in August,' his friend says, 'and left me $25,000.'

'Man, that's tough,' he replies.

'Then in September,' the friend continues, 'my father died, leaving me $90,000.'

'Wow. Two parents gone in two months. No wonder you're depressed.'

'And last month my aunt died, and left me $15,000.'

'Three close family members lost in three months? How sad.'

'Then this month,' continued the friend, 'absolutely nothing!'

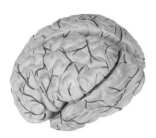

A BRAIN WALKS INTO A BAR and orders a pint of beer. The bartender says, 'I'm not serving you, you're out of your skull!'

A REGULAR CUSTOMER WALKS INTO A BAR one evening sporting a pair of swollen black eyes that look extremely painful.

'Hey, Sam!' says the bartender. 'Who gave you those beauties?'

'Nobody gave them to me,' said Sam. 'I had to fight like crazy for both of them.'

A MAN WALKS INTO A BAR, has a few drinks and asks what his tab is. The bartender replies that it is $20 plus tip. The man says, 'I'll bet you my tab double or nothing that I can bite my eye.' The bartender accepts the bet, and the man pulls out his glass eye and bites it.

He has a few more drinks and asks for his bill again. The bartender reports that his bill is now $30 plus tip. He bets the bartender he can bite his other eye. The bartender accepts, knowing the man can't possibly have two glass eyes. The man then proceeds to take out his false teeth and bite his other eye.

JOHN HURT WALKS INTO A BAR, with that alien emerging from his chest. The bartender asks, 'What's gotten into you?'

A MAN CALLED JOHN WALKS INTO HIS LOCAL PUB one day and orders his usual. He is enjoying a quiet pint at a table outside, when a nun suddenly appears at his table and starts decrying the evils of drink.

'You should be ashamed of yourself, young man! Drinking is a sin! Alcohol is the blood of the devil!'

Now John gets pretty annoyed about this, and goes on the offensive. 'How do you know this, Sister?'

'My Mother Superior told me so.'

'But have you ever had a drink yourself? How can you be sure that what you are saying is right?'

'Don't be ridiculous – of course I have never taken alcohol myself!'

'Then let me buy you a drink – if you still believe afterwards that it's evil I will give up drink for life.'

'How could I, a nun, sit outside this public house drinking?!'

'I'll get the bartender to put it in a teacup for you, then no one will ever know.'

The nun reluctantly agrees, so John goes inside to the bar. 'Another pint for me, and a triple vodka on the rocks,' then he lowers his voice and says to the bartender, 'and could you put the vodka in a teacup?'

'Oh no! It's not that nun again, is it?'

A COWBOY WALKS INTO A BAR and orders a large bourbon. Finishing his drink, he turns to face the guy playing the piano, takes out his gun, shoots the sheet music into the air, shoots the man's hat off and finally shoots the lid which falls down, trapping the poor man's fingers. He spins the gun and puts it back in its holster.

'Brilliant shooting,' says the bartender. 'Mind if I look at your gun?'

Another flashy spin brings the gun into the bartender's hands. 'Nice gun, but if I were you I would file off the sight, all the rough edges, and where your name is in diamonds on the handle, make it all nice and smooth.'

'What the hell for?' asks the cowboy.

'Well, see that piano player?' says the bartender. 'He is Billy the Kid, and when his hands are better he is going to ram that gun up where the sun don't shine.'

A MAN WALKS INTO A BAR and hurts his knee. What was that bar doing sticking up out of the ground?

A KID WALKS INTO A BAR.

'Hey, bartender. Pour me a cold one.'

'Hey, kid, you wanna get me in trouble?'

'Maybe later; right now I just want a beer.'

A FORKLIFT DRIVES INTO A BAR and raises a glass.

A MAN WALKS INTO A BAR and has a couple of beers. Once he is done the bartender tells him he owes $9.

'But I paid, don't you remember?' says the customer.

'OK,' says the bartender, 'If you say you paid, you did.'

The man then goes outside and tells the first person he sees that the bartender can't keep track of whether his customers have paid.

The second man then rushes in, orders a beer and later pulls the same stunt.

The barkeep replies, 'If you say you paid, I'll take your word for it.'

Soon the customer goes into the street, sees an old friend, and tells him how to get free drinks.

The man hurries into the bar and begins to drink highballs when, suddenly, the bartender leans over and says, 'You know, a funny thing happened in here tonight. Two men were drinking beer, neither paid and both claimed that they did. The next guy who tries that is going to get punched right in the nose.'

'Don't bother me with your troubles,' the final patron responds. 'Just give me my change and I'll be on my way.'

 DAVID HASSELHOFF WALKS INTO A BAR and says to the bartender, 'I want you to call me David Hoff.'

The bartender replies, 'Sure thing, Dave ... no hassle.'

 TWO DYSLEXICS WALK INTO A BRA ...

A MAN WALKS INTO A BAR in a remote Australian town. The newcomer hears people yell out numbers (23, 56 and so on) and then everyone laughs. He asks the bloke next to him what's going on, and he says the jokes have been told so many times before that people just yell out their numbers instead of retelling them. So the man yells out '27!', but nobody laughs.

The bloke next to him says, 'Some people can tell a joke, and some people can't.'

A MAN WALKS INTO A BAR and the bartender says to him, 'Hey, man, you've got a steering wheel down your pants.'

The man replies, 'Yeah, I know. It's driving me nuts!'

A MAN STOMPS INTO A BAR, obviously angry. He growls at the bartender, 'Gimme a beer,' takes a slug and shouts, 'All lawyers are arseholes!'

A bloke at the other end of the bar retorts, 'Take that back!'

The angry man snarls, 'Why? Are you a lawyer?'

The bloke replies, 'No, I'm an arsehole.'

CHARLES DICKENS WALKS INTO A BAR and orders a martini. The bartender asks, 'Olive or twist?'

A HUGE MAN WALKS INTO A BAR, and notices a little bloke sitting by himself drinking a beer. A while later he goes up to the little bloke and karate-chops him in the back. The little bloke falls off his barstool and when he gets up the big man says, 'That was a karate chop from Korea.'

The big man goes to the toilet and the little bloke orders himself another beer. About 20 minutes later the big man comes back and karate-chops the little bloke in the back again. The little bloke gets up and dusts himself off and the big man tells him, 'That was a karate chop from China.'

The little bloke gets up and decides he isn't going to take any more of this, so he leaves the bar. About an hour later the little bloke comes back in and hits the big man in the back. The big man is knocked out cold and he's on the floor. The little bloke tells the bartender, 'Tell him that was a crowbar from Bunnings!'

A PIECE OF ROPE WALKS INTO A BAR and the bartender says, 'We don't serve your kind.' The rope goes outside, ties himself in a knot and frays one of his ends. He walks back into the bar and the bartender says, 'Weren't you just in here?'

The rope replies, 'No, I'm a frayed knot.'

A MAN WALKS INTO A BAR with jumper leads. The bartender says, 'You can come in, but don't start anything!'

TWO HUNTERS WALK INTO A BAR at the same time every day. The first one always carries the skin of a bear; the other one is always empty-handed. So, one day the second man goes up to the first man and asks him how he manages to shoot a bear every day. 'Well, that's easy,' the first hunter replies. 'I just go over to one of those holes in the mountain, stand in front of it and shout "Yo, fat f***** of a bear, get your stinking arse out of this hole!" as loud as I can, then the bear comes out and I shoot it. Easy as that.'

'OK,' the other man says, 'I'll remember that.'

The next day the first hunter comes into the bar with his bearskin and orders a beer. About 10 minutes later the second one crawls in, covered in blood, missing a leg and generally looking a mess. The bartender yells, 'What the hell happened to you, man?!'

'Argh,' says the second hunter, ' I did what my buddy told me to do, I went to a hole, started shouting and swearing at that bear and guess what happened?'

'What?'

'A train came out.'

FOOD & DRINK

A GRILL WALKS INTO A BAR and toasts everybody.

A MAN WALKS INTO A BAR, sits down, and orders a drink. 'Hey, nice tie!' comes out of nowhere. He looks up at the bartender to see if he has said anything, but he is on the other side of the bar.

'Hey! Nice shirt!' The man looks up but, again, the bartender is engaged elsewhere.

'Hey! Nice suit!' The man then calls the bartender over and asks him if he has been talking to him.

'It's not me,' says the bartender, 'it's the complimentary nuts.'

TWO MEN WALK INTO A BAR and sit down to eat their lunches. The bartender says, 'Sorry, but you can't eat your own food in here.'

They look at each other, shrug, and swap lunches.

TWO TUBS OF YOGHURT WALK INTO A BAR. The bartender says, 'We don't serve your kind in here.'

'Why not? We're cultured!'

TWO PEANUTS WALK INTO A BAR. One was a salted.

AN OLD MAN WALKS INTO A BAR and asks for a bottle of 40-year-old Scotch. The bartender, not wanting to give up the good liquor, pours a shot of 10-year-old Scotch and figures that the man won't be able to tell the difference. The man downs the Scotch and says, 'This Scotch is only 10 years old! I specifically asked for 40-year-old Scotch.'

Amazed, the bartender reaches into a locked cabinet underneath the bar, pulls out a bottle of 20-year-old Scotch, and pours the man a shot. The man drinks it down and says, 'That was 20-year-old Scotch. I asked for 40-year-old Scotch.'

So the bartender goes into the back room, brings out a bottle of 30-year-old Scotch, and pours the man a drink. By now a small crowd has gathered around the man and is watching anxiously as he downs the latest drink. Once again the man states the true age of the Scotch and repeats his original request for 40-year-old Scotch.

The bartender can hold off no longer and disappears into the cellar to get a bottle of prime 40-year-old Scotch. Soon, the bartender returns with the bottle and pours a shot. The man downs the Scotch and says, 'Now this is 40-year-old Scotch!' The crowd applauds his discriminating palate.

An old drunk, who had been watching the proceedings with interest, raises a full shot glass of his own and says, 'Here, take a swig of this.'

The man takes the glass and downs the drink in one swallow. Immediately, he chokes and spits out the liquid on the floor. 'My God! That tastes like piss,' he yells.

'Great guess,' says the drunk. 'Now, how old am I?'

A MUSHROOM WALKS INTO A BAR and the bartender says, 'We don't serve your kind here.'

The mushroom says, 'Why not? I'm a fun-guy.'

A MAN WALKS INTO A BAR. The bartender says, 'Do you want to play a game? See those two T-bones nailed to the ceiling? You get to throw one dart. If you hit one, you get to take them home and I'll give you a free drink.'

The man says, 'No thanks, the steaks are too high.'

A MAN WALKS INTO A BAR. He says to the bartender, 'Can I have a bag of helicopter flavour chips?'

The bartender says, 'Sorry, we only have plain.'

AN EMPTY BEER BOTTLE WALKS INTO A BAR
and the bartender says, 'Hey, weren't you drunk
in here last night?'

A PICKLE WALKS INTO A BAR and the bartender
says, 'Hey, you're a pickle! What are you
doing here?'

The pickle says, 'Well, for starters, I'm
celebrating the fact that I can walk.'

BACON AND EGGS WALK INTO A BAR.
The bartender says, 'Sorry, we don't serve
breakfast.'

TWO CANNIBALS WALK INTO A BAR and sit beside a clown. The first cannibal whacks the clown on the head and they both start eating him. Suddenly the second cannibal looks up and says, 'Hey, do you taste something funny?'

THREE VAMPIRES WALK INTO A BAR and sit down. The first vampire says, 'I'd like a pint of blood.'

The second vampire says, 'I'd like a pint of blood, too.'

Then the third vampire says, 'I'd like a pint of plasma.'

Then the bartender says, 'OK, so let me get this straight, you want two bloods and a blood light?'

FIVE MEN WALK INTO A BAR. They're at a national conference of the Australian Hotels Association and they are the general managers of Cascade Brewery (Tasmania), Tooheys (New South Wales), XXXX (Queensland), CUB (Victoria) and Coopers (South Australia). They sit down at the same table for lunch.

When the waitress asks what they want to drink, the GM of Tooheys says without hesitation, 'I'll have a Tooheys New.'

The head of XXXX smiles and says, 'Make mine a XXXX Gold.'

To which the boss of Coopers rejoins, 'I'll have a Coopers, the King of Beers.'

And the bloke from Cascade asks for 'a Cascade, the cleanest draught on the planet'.

The General Manager of Carlton & United pauses a moment and then places his order: 'I'll have a Diet Coke.'

The others look at him as if he has sprouted a new head.

'Well,' he says with a shrug, 'if you wankers aren't drinking beer, neither will I.'

A BIG HULKING REDNECK WALKS INTO A BAR, slams his fist down and yells, 'Give me a VB, or …!' Scared, the bartender serves the man his VB. This happens every day for a week straight, and the bartender turns into a nervous wreck. He asks his wife for advice, and she tells him he should stand up for himself. Easier said than done, he thinks, but he decides to try it. The next day, the roughneck returns.

'Give me a VB, or …!'

'O-o-o-o-r-r-r w-what?' stammers the bartender.

'A small Coke.'

A HAMBURGER WALKS INTO A BAR. The bartender says, 'So what'll it be, Mac?'

A MAN WALKS INTO A BAR. He orders a pie and a pot. He sticks the pie on top of his head and twists and squashes it all over his head. He then downs his beer in one go and leaves.

Next day, same pub, same barman, same bloke comes in and repeats it all over again. The barman is lost for words and decides to get to the bottom of this strange habit next time the man comes in.

Next day, in walks the bloke and asks for his usual – a pie and a pot.

'Sorry,' says the barman. 'No pies left.'

'No problem,' says the man. 'I'll have a packet of chips instead. Oh, and a pot.'

The barman hands them over. The man sticks the chips on his head and twists and squashes them all over his head. Then he downs his beer in one go and gets up to leave.

'Oi,' shouts the barman. 'Why did you squash the chips all over your head? What's all that about then, eh?'

The bloke says, 'Well, you didn't have any pies left, did you!'

A CORNSTALK WALKS INTO A BAR. The
bartender says, 'Wanna hear a good joke?'

The cornstalk says, 'I'm all ears!'

A MAN WALKS INTO A BAR and orders a double.
The bartender brings out a bloke who looks just
like him.

A GHOST WALKS INTO A BAR at closing time.
The bartender says, 'Sorry, we don't serve
spirits at this time of night.'

A FLY WALKS INTO A BAR and orders a drink. The man next to him looks at him and says to the bartender, 'What's up with him?'

The bartender says, 'Oh, he works in the restaurant down the street.'

The man asks the fly, 'What line of work do you do?'

The fly sighs. 'I'm the one they put in the soup. It's exhausting.'

A MAN GOES INTO A BAR with a pork pie on his head. The bartender says, 'You've got a pork pie on your head.'

The man says, 'Yeah, I always wear a pork pie on my head on Wednesdays.'

The bartender says, 'It's only Tuesday!'

'Jesus, I must look like a right idiot then!' replies the man.

A POTATO WALKS INTO A BAR and all eyes are on him!

AN ENGLISHMAN, AN IRISHMAN, A SCOTSMAN, A RABBI, A MINISTER AND A PRIEST WALK INTO A BAR and the bartender says, 'What is this? Some kind of joke?'

A CANADIAN MAN WALKS INTO A BAR. On the stool next to his is some footwear. He says to the bartender, 'What's this – a boot?'

 SARAH JESSICA PARKER WALKS INTO A BAR and the bartender says, 'Why the long face?'

A MAN WALKS INTO A BAR and says, 'Give me three pints of Guinness, please.'

So the bartender brings him three pints and the man proceeds to sip one, then the next, and then the third until they're gone.

He then orders three more and the bartender says, 'Sir, I know you like them cold, so you can start with one and I'll bring you a fresh one as soon as you're low.'

The man says, 'You don't understand. I have two brothers: one in Australia, and one in the States. We made a vow to each other that every Saturday night we'd still drink together. So right now, my brothers have three Guinness stouts too and we're drinking together.'

The bartender thinks it's a wonderful tradition and every week he sets up the man's three beers as soon as he enters the bar. Then one week, the man comes in and orders only two. He drinks them, and then orders two more. The bartender says sadly, 'Knowing your tradition, I'd just like to say I'm sorry that one of your brothers died.'

The man replies, 'Oh, my brothers are fine – I just quit drinking.'

AN ELDERLY IRISHMAN WALKS INTO A BAR.
With great difficulty, he hoists his bad leg over a barstool, pulls himself up painfully and asks for a sip of Irish whisky.

The Irishman looks down the bar and asks, 'Is that Jesus over there?' The bartender nods, so the Irishman tells him to give Jesus an Irish whisky, too.

The next patron to come in is an ailing Italian with a hunched back, who moves very slowly. He shuffles up to a barstool and asks for a glass of chianti.

He also looks down the bar and asks, 'Is that Jesus sitting at the end of the bar?' The bartender nods, so the Italian says to give Him a glass of chianti, too.

The third patron to enter the bar is a redneck, who swaggers into the bar and hollers, 'Barkeep, set me up a cold one!'

'Hey, is that God's Boy down there?' the redneck asks.

The barkeep nods, so the redneck tells him to give Jesus a cold one, too.

As Jesus gets up to leave, he walks over to the Irishman, touches him, and says, 'For your kindness, you are healed!' The Irishman feels the strength come back to his leg, so he gets up and dances a jig out the door.

Jesus touches the Italian and says, 'For your kindness, you are healed!' The Italian feels his back straighten, so he raises his hands above his head and does a flip out the door.

Jesus walks towards the redneck, but the redneck jumps back and exclaims, 'Don't touch me! I'm on a disability pension!'

A MAN WALKS INTO A BAR and says, 'I've got a Kiwi joke to tell.'

The bartender replies, 'I'm 6'4", 130kg, and I played in the second row for the All Blacks two years ago. See the other bartender? He's 6'6", 140kg, and played for the All Blacks four years ago. And see the man collecting the glasses? He's 5'10", 125kg, and currently plays tight head prop for the All Blacks. You still want to tell that joke?'

To which the man replies, 'Not if I've got to explain it three times!'

A MAN WALKS INTO A BAR. 'Pint of your best,' he says to the barman. While waiting for his drink he notices that Vincent van Gogh is sitting at one of the tables. He goes up to him and says, 'Are you Vincent van Gogh?'

'Yes,' the old man replies.

'Do you want a pint?' the man asks.

'No, ta,' Vincent replies. 'I've got one 'ere.'

A MAN WALKS INTO A BAR in Cork, Ireland, and asks the barman, 'What's the quickest way to get to Dublin?'

'Are you walking or driving?' asks the barman.

'Driving,' says the man.

'That's the quickest way,' says the barman.

AN ENGLISHMAN, A SCOTSMAN AND AN IRISHMAN WALK INTO A BAR and order a round of beers. When the beers arrive, each one has a fly floating on top.

The Englishman sends his back in disgust.

The Scotsman flicks the fly out and starts to drink his pint.

The Irishman holds up the fly and screams, 'SPIT IT OUT! SPIT IT OUT!'

A TEXAN, A CALIFORNIAN AND A SEATTLEITE WALK INTO A BAR at the same time. After a while, the Texan grabs a bottle of tequila, throws it in the air and shoots it into a thousand pieces. 'Don't you boys worry about it,' says the Texan, 'we have plenty of tequila deep in the heart of Texas.'

The Californian, not wanting to be outdone, selects a bottle of fine wine, tosses it up, and shoots it into smithereens. 'Hey, don't sweat it dudes,' chirps the Californian. 'There're zillions of bottles of wine in Cal.'

The Seattleite, following suit, guzzles down a bottle of micro-brewed beer, chucks it towards the rafters, shoots the Californian and, without missing a beat, puts out his hand and catches the beer bottle. Everyone in the bar stands frozen in shock.

'Relax, kids,' says the Seattleite coolly. 'Up in Seattle, there's a freakin' shipload of Californians. No big deal.'

A FARMER WALKS INTO A BAR in New Zealand with the fluffiest sheep you've ever seen. The wool would weigh more than the sheep – it drags on the ground under the sheep's belly and covers its eyes.

The bartender asks, 'Are you gonna shear that sheep?'

The farmer replies, 'I am not shearing her with anyone, she is mine and I love her!'

TWO ATOMS WALK INTO A BAR. One of them says, 'Damn – I think I've lost an electron!'

The other atom asks, 'Are you sure?'

'Yeah, I'm positive.'

A MAN WALKS INTO A BAR, stumbles up to the only other patron and asks if he can buy him a drink. 'Why of course,' comes the reply.

The first man then asks, 'Where are you from?'

'I'm from Ireland,' replies the second man.

The first man responds, 'You don't say, I'm from Ireland too! Let's have another round to Ireland.'

'Of course,' replies the second man.

'I'm curious,' the first man says. 'Where in Ireland are you from?'

'Dublin,' comes the reply.

'I can't believe it,' says the first man. 'I'm from Dublin too! Let's have another drink to Dublin.'

'Of course,' replies the second man.

Curiosity again strikes and the first man asks, 'What school did you go to?'

'Saint Mary's,' replies the second man. 'I graduated in '62.'

'This is unbelievable!' the first man says. 'I went to Saint Mary's and I graduated in '62, too!'

About that time one of the regulars comes in and sits down at the bar. 'What's been going on?' he asks the bartender.

'Nothing much,' replies the bartender. 'The O'Kinly twins are drunk again.'

A NORTHERNER WALKS INTO A BAR in the Deep South around Christmas time. A small nativity scene is behind the bar, and the guy says, 'That's a nice nativity scene. But how come the three wise men are all wearing firemen's hats?'

'Well, it says right there in the Bible: the three wise men came from a-far,' drawls the bartender.

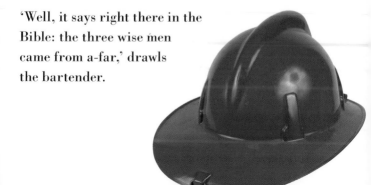

AN AUSSIE AND A KIWI WALK INTO A BAR. They have quite a few drinks.

The Aussie says, 'If I sneak over to your place and make wild passionate love to your wife and she gets pregnant and has a baby, would that make us related?'

The Kiwi scratches his head, thinking long and hard about his friend's question.

Finally, he says, 'Well, I don't know about related, bro, but it sure would make us even!'

 A WOMAN GOES INTO A BAR and asks for a 'double entendre'. So the bartender gives her one.

A TEXAN WALKS INTO A BAR in Ireland
and clears his voice to address the crowd of
drinkers. He says, 'I hear you Irish are damn
good drinkers. I'll give 500 American dollars
to anybody in here who can drink 10 pints of
Guinness back-to-back.'

The room is quiet and no one takes up the
Texan's offer. One man even leaves. Thirty
minutes later the same gentleman who left shows
back up and taps the Texan on the shoulder.
'Is your bet still good?' asks the Irishman.

The Texan says yes and asks the bartender to
line up 10 pints of Guinness. Immediately the
Irishman tears into the pint glasses, drinking
them all back-to-back.

The other patrons cheer as the Texan watches in
amazement.

The Texan gives the Irishman the $500 and says,
'If you don't mind me askin', where did you go
for the past 30 minutes?'

The Irishman replies, 'Oh ... I had to go to the
pub down the street to see if I could do it first.'

A JEWISH MAN WALKS INTO A BAR and sits down beside a Chinese man. All of a sudden the Jew turns and punches the Chinese in the face, knocking him off his stool. Stunned, the Chinese man gets up and says, 'What the hell was that for?'

The Jew replies, 'That was for Pearl Harbour.'

The Chinese man says, 'That was the Japanese, I'm Chinese.'

The Jew says, 'Well, you have black hair, squinty eyes and buckteeth, it's all the same to me.'

The Chinese man says, 'OK,' sits back on his stool and continues drinking.

Half an hour later the Chinese man turns and punches the Jew in the face, knocking him off his stool. The Jew gets up and says, 'What the hell was that for?'

The Chinese man says, 'That was for the Titanic.'

The Jew replies, 'The Titanic? That was an iceberg.'

The Chinese man says, 'Iceberg, Goldberg, Steinberg, it's all the same to me.'

A FRENCHMAN WALKS INTO A BAR with a parrot on his shoulder. The parrot is wearing a baseball cap. The bartender says, 'Hey, that's cool – where did you get that?'

And the parrot says, 'France – they've got millions of them there.'

A MAN WALKS INTO A BAR one night and gets really drunk. Really, really, really drunk. When the bar closes he gets up to go home. As he stumbles out the door he sees a nun walking on the footpath.

So he stumbles across to the nun and trips her over. Then he leans down, puts his face right next to hers and says, 'Not very strong tonight are you, Batman?'

A SCOTSMAN, AN ENGLISHMAN AND AN IRISHMAN WALK INTO A BAR and begin discussing the best pubs around. The Englishman says, 'There's a pub in the West Midlands where the landlord buys you a drink for every one that you buy.'

The Scot is not impressed and says, 'That's nothing! In the Highlands every time you buy a drink the landlord buys you five.'

At this point the Englishman is fairly impressed.

The Irishman, totally unimpressed, says, 'That's nothing. In Dublin there's this pub where the landlord buys your drinks all night, and then when the bar shuts he takes you into a room and makes love to you.'

The Scot and the Englishman are well impressed and ask if the Irishman goes there a lot. He replies, 'No, but my sister told me about it.'

ALL CREATURES GREAT AND SMALL

**A DUCK WALKS INTO
A BAR** and says,
'Got any bread?'

The bartender says, 'No.'

The duck says, 'Got any bread?'

The bartender says, 'NO!'

'Got any bread?'

'I said N-O, NO!'

'Got any bread?'

'For crying out loud – N-O spells NO,
and I mean NO!'

'Got any bread?'

'NO NO NO NO NO NO NO NO NO NO NO NO NO!'

'Got any bread?'

'Look, if you ask me one more f***ing time if I've got any bread, I'm going to nail your f***ing beak to the f**ing bar!'

'Got any nails?'

'No.'

'Got any bread?'

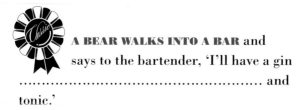 **A BEAR WALKS INTO A BAR** and says to the bartender, 'I'll have a gin .... and tonic.'

'What's with the big pause?' the bartender asks.

'I don't know,' the bear says. 'My dad had them too.'

A 6-FOOT TALL COCKROACH WALKS INTO A BAR. He punches the bartender in the face and leaves. The next day the bruised bartender finds himself staring at the same cockroach. The cockroach kicks him in the shin and pokes his eye out and then leaves. The next day the battered bartender sees the same cockroach standing at the bar again. The cockroach stabs him several times and leaves. This time the bartender drags himself to the phone and calls the police. He is taken to the nearest hospital and kept there overnight. The next day the doctor comes in to talk to the man.

'Tell me, son,' the doctor says, 'what happened last night? These injuries are pretty vicious.'

'I was attacked by a 6-foot cockroach!' the bartender replies.

'Aha,' says the doctor. 'I heard there was a nasty bug going around.'

A GIRAFFE WALKS INTO A BAR and says, 'High balls are on me!'

A SHEEP WALKS INTO A BAAAAAA.

A GOLDFISH WALKS INTO A BAR and looks at the bartender. The bartender asks, 'What can I get you?'

The goldfish says, 'Water.'

A HORSE WALKS INTO A BAR, across the room, up the back wall, across the ceiling, down the front wall and then up to the bar. The bartender gives the horse a beer; he drinks it and leaves. A man sitting at the bar looks perplexed and asks the bartender, 'Hey, what's that all about?'

The bartender replies, 'Don't take it personally, he never says "Hi" to anyone.'

A KANGAROO HOPS INTO A BAR. He orders a beer. The bartender says, 'That'll be $10. You know, we don't get many kangaroos in here.'

The kangaroo says, 'At $10 a beer, that's not hard to understand!'

A CIRCUS OWNER WALKS INTO A BAR to see everyone crowded around a table watching a little show. On the table is an upside down pot and a duck tap-dancing on it. The circus owner is so impressed that he offers to buy the duck from its owner. After some wheeling and dealing they settle on $10,000 for the duck and the pot.

Three days later the circus owner runs back to the bar in anger. 'Your duck is a rip-off! I put him on the pot before a whole audience, and he didn't dance a single step!'

'So,' asks the duck's former owner, 'did you remember to light the candle under the pot?'

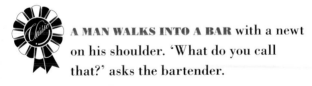

A MAN WALKS INTO A BAR with a newt on his shoulder. 'What do you call that?' asks the bartender.

'I call him Tiny, because he's my newt!'

A MAN WALKS INTO A BAR with a duck on his head. The bartender says, 'Hey, where did you get that?'

The duck answers, 'Outside, there's thousands of 'em!'

A RABBIT WALKS INTO A BAR and orders a Guinness. When he gets it the rabbit shouts out, 'Cheeeeeeeeeeeeeeers!'

'Why the long ears?' asks the girl behind the bar.

HUH?

A BEAR WALKS INTO A BAR one hot summer's day and asks the man behind the bar for a beer. The bartender tells the bear that they don't serve bears at this bar. The bear says that he is tired and thirsty and not in a good mood so if he doesn't get a beer he will eat one of the patrons. The bartender refuses to serve him, so the bear eats a beautiful blonde in the corner and walks back to the bar and says that if he doesn't get a beer he'll eat another patron.

The bartender tells him that they never serve drug addicts in this bar. The bear says, 'Drug addict? What are you talking about?'

The bartender says, 'That was a barbiturate.'

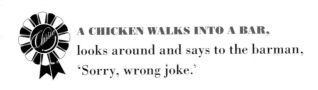 **A CHICKEN WALKS INTO A BAR,** looks around and says to the barman, 'Sorry, wrong joke.'

A MAN WALKS INTO A BAR. A horse is behind the bar serving drinks. The man stares at the horse, who says, 'What are you staring at? Haven't you ever seen a horse serving drinks before?'

The man says, 'No, I never thought the parrot would sell the place.'

A MAN WALKS INTO A BAR holding a crocodile. He asks the bartender, 'Do you serve lawyers here?'

The bartender says, 'Yes, we do!'

'Good,' replies the man. 'Give me a beer, and I'll have a lawyer for my crocodile.'

A COW WALKS INTO A BAR and says, 'Hay, bartender!'

A MAN WALKS INTO A BAR and asks the bartender if he will give him a free beer if he shows him something amazing. The bartender agrees, so the man pulls out a hamster, which begins dancing and singing 'Yellow Submarine' by The Beatles.

'That *is* amazing!' says the bartender and gives the man his free beer.

'If I show you something else amazing, will you give me another beer?' The bartender agrees, so the man pulls out a small piano and a frog. Now the hamster plays the piano while the frog dances and sings 'Uptown Girl' by Billy Joel. The bartender, completely wowed, gives him another beer. A man in a suit, who's been watching the entire time, offers to buy the frog for a princely sum, which the man agrees to.

'Are you nuts?' asks the bartender. 'You could've made a fortune out of that frog.'

'Can you keep a secret?' asks the man.
'The hamster's a ventriloquist.'

A MAN WALKS INTO A BAR, very down on himself. As he walks up to the bar the bartender asks, 'What's the matter?'

The fellow replies, 'Well, I've got these two horses (sniff, sniff), and well … I can't tell them apart. I don't know if I'm mixing up riding times or even feeding them the right foods.'

The bartender, feeling sorry for the man, tries to think of something he can do. 'Why don't you try shaving the tail of one of the horses?'

The man stops crying and says, 'Hey, thanks, that sounds like a good idea, I think I'll try it.'

A few months later he comes back to the bar in worse condition than he was before. 'What's the matter now?' the bartender asks.

The fellow, in no condition to be out in public, answers, 'I shaved the tail of one of the horses (sob, sob), but it grew back and I can't tell them apart again!'

The bartender, now just wanting him to shut up or leave, says, 'Why don't you try shaving the mane, maybe that won't grow back.'

The fellow stops crying, has a few drinks, and leaves.

A few months later the fellow is back in the bar. The bartender has never seen anybody in this sorry a state. Without the bartender even asking, the fellow breaks into a chorus of his problems. 'I, I shaved the (sob) mane of one of the (sniff) horses, and it … it … grew back!'

The bartender, now furious at the man's general stupidity, yells, 'For crying out loud, just measure the stupid horses. Perhaps one is slightly taller that the other one!' The fellow cannot believe what the bartender has said and storms out of the bar.

The next day the fellow comes running back into the bar as if he has just won the lottery. 'It worked, it worked!' he exclaims. 'I measured the horses and the black one is two inches taller than the white one!'

A MAN WALKS INTO A BAR holding three ducks. He sets them on the bar and orders a drink. After talking with the bartender for a while, the man excuses himself to use the toilet. The bartender feels a bit awkward with just himself and three ducks at the bar, so he tries to make small talk with them.

He asks the first duck, 'What's your name?'

'Huey,' replies the duck.

'So, how's your day been?'

'Oh, I've had a great day,' replies Huey. 'I've been in and out of puddles all day.'

The bartender asks the second duck, 'What's your name?'

'Dewey,' replies the duck.

'So, how's your day been?'

'Oh, I've had a great day,' replies Dewey. 'I've been in and out of puddles all day.'

The witty bartender says to the third duck, 'So I guess your name is Louie?'

The duck replies, 'No, I'm Puddles.'

A MAN WALKS INTO A BAR and offers to do his act in exchange for a few beers. When asked by the bartender what his act is, he tells him that he can fart the national anthem. Thinking that this will be worth a listen the bartender agrees, gives the man his beers and watches as the man approaches the stage. The man takes off his pants ... and takes a dump right on the stage.

'What the hell are you doing?' shouts the bartender. 'I thought you were going to fart the national anthem!'

'I am,' replies the man, 'but even Frank Sinatra cleared his throat first!'

 A MAN WALKS INTO A BAR ... Ouch!

A MAN WALKS INTO A BAR and slips over on a pile of vomit. Minutes later a huge, hairy bikie walks in and slips over on the same pile of vomit.

The first man says to the bikie, 'Hey, I just did that!' and the bikie promptly king-hits him.

A MAN WALKS INTO A BAR and buys a Guinness. He is just about to take a sip when a pianist in the corner of the room suddenly starts playing a frantic tune; the pianist's dancing monkey promptly leaps from the piano, across the bar and dunks his scrotum in the customer's Guinness!

Disgusted, the man puts down his glass and approaches the pianist.

'Do you know your monkey dunked his balls in my pint?'

'No, but if you hum it I'll play it,' came the reply.

A MAN WALKS INTO A BAR, pulls out a tiny piano and stool, and a tiny little man. The tiny man sits down, and starts to play the piano. Another man notices and asks, 'Hey, what's that?'

'A 12-inch pianist. You see, I found this magic lamp, rubbed it, made a wish and I got a 12-inch pianist.'

'Can I try?' The man with the piano agrees and a minute later, a million ducks fill the room.

'Ducks? I didn't wish for a million ducks, I wished for a million bucks!'

'You think I really wished for a 12-inch pianist?'

A MAN CALLED FRANK WALKS INTO A BAR. He's had a few drinks when the bartender comes over to tell him that he has a telephone call. Frank has just bought another beer and he doesn't want anyone else to drink it. So, he writes a little sign and leaves it by his beer: 'I spat in my beer.'

When Frank returns to his bar stool, there is another note beside his beer: 'I spat in your beer, too!'

A WELL-TO-DO COUPLE WALK INTO A BAR and sit down next to a drunk. Suddenly, the drunk lets out a tremendously loud fart.

'Excuse me! How dare you fart before my wife!' the man yells.

'Oh, sorry,' the drunk slurs. 'I didn't know it was her turn.'

TWO MEN WALK INTO A BAR, one wearing a cowboy hat and the other wearing a Holden cap. The man in the Holden cap approaches the bartender and makes a bet: 'I'll bet you $1000 that I can put a shot glass at one end of your bar and piss into it from the other end of the bar without spilling a drop.'

The bartender laughs and says, 'You're crazy, but you're on.'

The man positions a shot glass on one end of the bar, walks to the other end and unzips his fly. He then pisses everywhere – all over the walls, over the bar top, all over the bottles of booze, and all over the bartender. The bartender roars with laughter and tells the man to pay up.

The man in the Holden cap pays up, laughing and smiling, too.

'What are you smiling at?' asks the bartender. 'You just lost $1000!'

'Well, you see that guy in the cowboy hat over there crying? Before we came in, I bet him $10,000 that I could piss all over your bar, your walls, your liquor *and* you, and not only would you not be mad – you would laugh hysterically about it!'

A MAN WALKS INTO A BAR and gets very drunk. He heads for the toilet. A few minutes later, there's a blood-curdling scream. A few minutes after that, another loud scream echoes around the bar. The bartender goes to investigate. 'What's all the screaming about in there?' he yells. 'You're scaring my customers!'

The drunk responds, 'I'm just sitting here on the toilet and every time I try to flush, something comes up and squeezes the hell out of my balls.'

The bartender opens the door and looks in. 'You idiot!' he says. 'You're sitting on the mop bucket!'

JESUS CHRIST WALKS INTO A BAR, slams three nails down onto the counter and says to the bartender, 'Can you put me up for the night?'

AN ALIEN WALKS INTO A BAR and sits next to a drunk bloke and begins poking him in the shoulder. The drunk just ignores him. After a while the bloke turns to the alien and begins looking him up and down. He notices that the alien has no genitalia. So he asks, 'If you guys have no genitalia, how do you have sex?'

The alien, still poking him in the arm, just smiles!

A FLY WALKS INTO A BAR and goes up to a woman sitting at the bar and says, 'I like that stool you're sitting on.'

TWO MEN WALK INTO A BAR. The third one ducks.

TWO OLD BLOKES WALK INTO A BAR and have a few drinks. When they stagger out a couple of hours later, one of them almost falls over a dog on the footpath. The dog is licking his balls.

The old bloke looks at his mate, smiles and says, 'I wish I could do that!'

His mate says, 'Don't you think you should pat him and get to know him first?'

HUH?

TWO POLYNOMIALS WALK INTO A BAR. The bartender, a derivative, asks them, 'Can I take your order?'

The polynomials run out screaming, 'Help! The bartender threatened to kill me!'

THREE HOBOS WALK INTO A BAR. The first one asks for a fork. The second one also asks for a fork. Then the third one wants a straw. At this point, the bartender becomes curious. 'How come both your friends want forks and you want a straw?'

'Well,' the bum says, 'the dog threw up and the chunks are all gone.'

SHAKESPEARE WALKS INTO A BAR and asks the bartender for a beer. 'I can't serve you,' says the bartender. 'You're Bard!'

AN ARMLESS MAN WALKS INTO A BAR
which is empty except for the bartender.
He orders a drink and when he has been
served, asks the bartender if he would mind
getting the money from his wallet in his pocket,
since he has no arms. The bartender obliges.
Next the man asks if the bartender would tip
the glass to his lips. The bartender holds the
glass until the man finishes his drink. The
man then asks if the bartender would get a
hanky from his pocket and wipe the foam from
his lips. The bartender does it and comments
that it must be very difficult to have no arms
and have to ask someone to do nearly everything
for you.

The man says, 'Yes, it is a bit embarrassing
at times. By the way, where's the toilet?'

The bartender quickly replies, 'The closest
one is in the service station three blocks down
the street.'

A MAN WALKS INTO A BAR and sits down. He starts dialling numbers like there's a telephone in his hand, then puts his palm up against his cheek and begins talking. Suspicious, the bartender walks over and tells him that this is a very tough neighbourhood and he doesn't need any trouble.

The man says, 'You don't understand. I'm very hi-tech. I had a phone installed in my hand because I was tired of carrying my mobile.'

The bartender says, 'Prove it.'

The man dials up a number and holds his hand out to the bartender. The bartender talks into the hand and carries on a conversation.

'That's incredible!' says the bartender. 'I would never have believed it!'

'Yeah,' says the man, 'I can keep in touch with my broker, my wife, you name it. By the way, where is the men's room?'

The bartender directs him to the men's room. The man goes in and 5, 10, 20 minutes go by and he doesn't return. Fearing the worst, given the area, the bartender goes into the men's room to check on the man. The man is spread-eagled up against the wall. His pants are pulled down and he has a roll of toilet paper up his butt.

'Oh my God!' says the bartender. 'Did they rob you? Are you hurt?'

The man turns and says:
'No, no, I'm OK.
I'm just waiting
for a fax.'

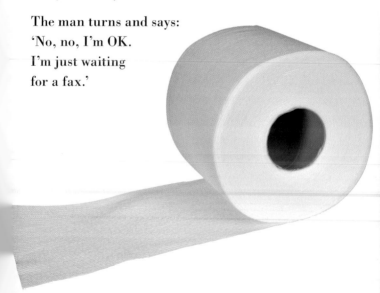

A MAN WALKS INTO A BAR and sits on a stool. In front of him he sees a big jar full of change and a little card that reads: 'Hello, if you would like to win all of this money you have to make the horse at the end of the bar laugh. COST $5'

So, he puts in $5 and takes the horse into the bathroom. Two minutes later they come out and the horse is laughing so hard that he pisses on the floor. The man takes the money and leaves.

The next day the same man walks into the bar again and sees the horse and the jar. This time the card says: 'You can win all of this if you make the horse cry. COST $10'

So he puts in $10 and takes the horse into the bathroom. Four minutes later they come out and the horse is crying like his heart is breaking. The man takes the jar but before he can leave the bartender asks, 'How did you do that?'

The man says, 'The first time I told him my dick was bigger than his and the second time I showed him!'

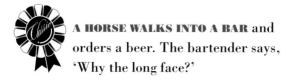

A HORSE WALKS INTO A BAR and orders a beer. The bartender says, 'Why the long face?'

THREE MEN WALK INTO A BAR and the bartender says, 'If you can sit in my basement for a day I'll give you free beer forever.'

So the first man says, 'Easy. I can do that.'

But he walks out after five minutes and says, 'It's impossible, you got a swarm of flies in there.'

So the second man tries his luck, but can't take it for more than 10 minutes. Finally the third man goes in and comes out a day later. The others ask him how he did it.

He said, 'Easy. I took a dump in one corner and sat in the other corner!'

AN ENGLISHMAN STAGGERS INTO A BAR in Queensland. It's the middle of summer and he's been caught in a huge tropical storm, riding a bicycle. He looks like a drowned rat. The locals hardly even look up from their beers as he walks in and heads up to the bar to order a Scotch on ice. The barman gives him the worst Scotch he has ever tasted but the Englishman drinks it down and asks the barman where the dunny is. The barman tells him it is outside.

So the Englishman trudges outside into the rain and all he can see is two big piles of pooh, one much bigger than the other. So he walks over to the smaller pile, relieved that someone had the sense to start a new pile since the larger one is clearly unmanageable.

He has his pants around his ankles and is in the process of relieving himself when a gunshot rings out and a bullet smacks into the heap just beside his head.

The poor Englishman turns around, in a somewhat vulnerable position, and sees this huge Aussie bloke standing at the door of the pub with his still-smoking gun in his hand.

'What ... what's going on?' he stammers.

The huge Aussie responds, 'Get the hell out of the Ladies, you dirty bastard.'

HUH?

DESCARTES WALKS INTO A BAR. The bartender asks, 'Would you like a beer?'

Descartes replies, 'I think not,' then disappears.

A MAN WALKS INTO A BAR on the top floor of the largest skyscraper in town. He takes a seat. Another man walks in and asks the bartender for a Jack Daniels. He downs it, and then takes a running leap out the window. Much to everybody's surprise, he floats back up and climbs through the window back into the bar. The man at the bar is amazed and asks the man how he did it.

'Easy,' says the man. 'Outside this window are some very strong wind currents which can carry you back up.'

'Wow,' says the man at the bar. 'I gotta try this.' He takes a running leap out the window and falls to a horrible, bloody, flat death.

'Geez, Superman,' says the bartender.
'You can be a real prick when you're drunk.'

A FEW
TOO
MANY ...

A MAN WALKS INTO A BAR. He drinks a lot. The bartender tosses him out for being too drunk. The drunk walks back into the bar. Again, the bartender throws him out for being too drunk. Again the drunk walks into the bar. The bartender is just about to throw him out when the drunk looks at him and says, 'How many bars do you own, anyway?'

A MAN WALKS INTO A BAR and says, 'Give me a beer before problems start!' He drinks the beer, then orders another, saying, 'Give me a beer before problems start!'

The bartender looks confused. This goes on for a while, and after the fifth beer the bartender is totally confused and asks the man, 'When are you going to pay for these beers?'

The man answers, 'Ah, now the problems start!'

A MAN WALKS INTO A BAR and orders a whisky. He sits down and just before he takes a sip a bloke runs in and says, 'Bill! Your house burnt down!'

So he runs outside but then he thinks, 'I don't have a house.' So he goes back into the bar and takes a sip of his whisky.

Another bloke runs in and says, 'Bill! Your dad died!'

And so he runs out of the bar, heads down the road but then thinks, 'I don't have a dad.'

So he goes back into the bar and drinks almost all of his whisky, when another bloke runs in and says, 'Bill! You won the lottery!'

So he runs out, and heads down the road all the way to the bank but then thinks, 'My name's not Bill.'

A MAN WALKS INTO A BAR after work and by 2am he is extremely drunk. When he enters his house, he doesn't want to wake anyone, so he takes off his shoes and starts tiptoeing up the stairs. Halfway up the stairs he falls over backwards and lands flat on his arse. That wouldn't be so bad, except that he has a couple of spare stubbies in his back pockets, and they break and carve up his backside. He's so drunk that he doesn't know he's hurt.

A few minutes later, as he's undressing, he notices blood, so he checks himself out in the mirror, and, sure enough, his backside is all carved up. He repairs the damage as best he can under the circumstances, and goes to bed.

The next morning his head is hurting, his bum is hurting, and he's hiding under the covers trying to think up some good story when his wife comes into the bedroom.

'Well, you really tried one on last night,' she says. 'Where'd you go?'

'I worked late,' he says, 'and I stopped off for a couple of beers.'

'A couple of beers? That's a laugh,' she replies. 'You got plastered last night. Where the heck did you go?'

'What makes you so sure I got drunk last night, anyway?'

'Well,' she replies, 'my first big clue was when I got up this morning and found a bunch of bandaids stuck to the mirror.'

TWO NIPPLES WALK INTO A BAR. The barman says, 'I'm not serving you, you're off your tits.'

HUH?

TWO ALPHA PARTICLES AND A GAMMA RAY WALK INTO A BAR ... magnet.

A MAN WALKS INTO A BAR wearing a neck brace and asks for a pint. The bartender says OK. Then the man asks who's in the lounge. And the bartender says, 'Fifteen people playing darts.' So the man says to get them a pint too.

Then he asks who's upstairs and the bartender says there are 150 people having a disco. The man says to get them a drink too.

The bartender says, 'That will be $328, please.'

And the man says, 'Sorry but I haven't got that much money on me.'

The bartender says, 'If you were down in the pub a mile from here, they would have broken your neck.'

The man says, 'I've already been there.'

TWO MEN WALK INTO A BAR and order drinks. While they're waiting they watch the news on TV. It shows a man on a bridge who is about to jump, obviously suicidal. 'I bet you $10 he'll jump,' says the first man.

'Bet you $10 he won't,' says the second man.

Then, the man on the television closes his eyes and throws himself off the bridge. The second man hands the first man the money.

'I can't take your money,' the first man says. 'I cheated you. The same story was on the 5 o'clock news.'

'No, no. Take it,' says the second man. 'I saw the 5 o'clock news too. I just didn't think the man was dumb enough to jump again!'

A MAN WALKS INTO A BAR and staggers out drunk several hours later. He runs right into two priests. He says, 'I'm Jesus Christ.' The first priest says, 'No, son, you're not.' So the drunk says it to the second priest. The second priest says, 'No, son, you're not.' The drunk says, 'Look, I can prove it.' He walks back into the bar with the two priests. The bartender takes one look at the drunk and exclaims, 'Jesus Christ, you're here again?'

A MAN WALKS INTO A BAR and starts drinking quite heavily. After a while he starts bothering the barman about the airconditioning – first he asks for the airconditioning to be turned up because it is too hot, then he asks for it to be turned down because it is too cold. This goes on for a couple of hours. To the surprise of other drinkers in the bar, the barman is very patient, walking back and forth and being very accommodating. Finally a man at the bar asks, 'Why don't you just throw him out?'

'Oh, I don't care,' says the barman with a grin. 'We don't actually have an airconditioner here.'

A MAN WALKS INTO A BAR, orders 12 shots and starts drinking them as fast as he can.

The bartender asks, 'Why are you drinking so fast?'

The man says, 'You'd be drinking fast too if you had what I had.'

The bartender says, 'What do you have?'

The man says, '75 cents.'

A MAN WALKS INTO A BAR and asks the barman, 'Was I in here last night?'

'You certainly were,' replies the barman.

'And did I spend a lot of money?'

'You spent over $100,' replies the barman.

'Thank God for that,' says the man, 'I thought I'd wasted it.'

A MAN WALKS INTO A BAR on his way to buy
some escargot for a fancy French dinner party
he and his wife are having that night. He has
a few beers, and then some more, and pretty
soon he looks at his watch and finds he's over
an hour late for the dinner party. He dashes to
the gourmet food store, picks up the escargot
and frantically drives home. When he walks
in the door he can hear his wife coming from
the kitchen. So he takes the bag of snails and
quickly throws them all over the floor. When
his wife walks into the room he says, 'Come on
guys, we're almost there!'

A MAN WALKS INTO A BAR and orders a beer. The bartender puts a coaster and a beer on the bar. Ten minutes later the man orders another beer. The bartender brings him the beer and sees that that coaster has disappeared, so he brings another one. Ten minutes later, another beer, and again the coaster is missing. This time the bartender puts the beer down without a coaster.

'Hey,' the man says, 'what about my cookie?'

A MAN WALKS INTO A BAR with a roll of bitumen under his arm and says, 'A beer please, and one for the road.'

A MAN WALKS INTO A BAR. 'A beer please, bartender, and one for yourself,' he says.

'Why, thank you, sir,' says the bartender. 'That'll be $8.50.'

'Can I run up a tab?'

'Certainly, sir.'

The man comes back. 'Another pint please, and whatever you're having.'

'Thank you, sir!'

Again he comes back and offers the bartender another drink plus some for a few people sitting nearby.

Yet again he comes back and offers to get everyone at the bar a drink.

'Last orders, gentlemen!'

'Get everyone in the place a drink and make it a double!'

The time comes to settle up.

'But I haven't got any money,' says the man.

Enraged, the bartender beats the shit out of him and breaks his arm. The next day when the bar opens the same man hobbles up to the bar on crutches with his arm in plaster. 'I'll have a beer, whatever these people are having, but nothing for you – you turn nasty after a few drinks!'

HUH?

EINSTEIN WALKS INTO A BAR and says to the bartender, 'I'll take a beer and a beer for my friend, Heisenberg.'

The bartender looks around and asks, 'Is your friend here?'

'Well,' says Einstein, 'he is and he isn't.'

A MAN WALKS INTO A BAR and orders a drink.
He notices a drunk who keeps falling off his
stool. The man finishes his drink watching the
other man trying to get back up on the stool.
Feeling a bit sorry for the drunk, the man tries
to help him stand up, but the drunk keeps
falling. The man offers the drunk a lift home,
but the drunk can't speak so the man finds his
address in his wallet. On the way to the car,
the man has to practically carry the drunk.
At the drunk's house, he pulls into the drive
way and half-carries, half-drags the man to the
front door. He rings the doorbell and a woman
answers the door.

'Ma'am, your husband is very drunk so
I decided to give him a lift home.'

'That's very kind of you,' says the woman.
'Thank you, but ... where's his wheelchair?'

MORE
CREATURES
GREAT
AND
SMALL

A MAN WALKS INTO A BAR holding a duck. The bartender says, 'Mate, whaddaya doing with that pig?'

'This ain't no pig,' says the customer. 'It's a duck.'

'I wasn't talking to you,' the bartender says, 'I was talking to the duck.'

A DUCK WALKS INTO A BAR and sits down at the counter. 'Bartender!' he says. 'Let me have a dry martini, just put it on my bill!'

A CROCODILE WALKS INTO A BAR and orders a schnapps.

FRED AND HIS BROTHER, 'DONKEY', WALK INTO A BAR. Fred gets the first round in and says, 'I'll have a pint for me and a pint for Donkey.'

The two men drink their pints and Fred says, 'Right, Donkey, your round. I'll have a pint of Guinness.'

Donkey walks up to the bar and says, 'Two p— pints of G— Guinness p— please.'

While Donkey gets the pints, Fred goes to the toilet and the bartender says, 'You know, you shouldn't let him call you that stupid nickname.'

Donkey replies, 'I know. He aw—, he aw—, he awwwwww—, he always calls me Donkey.'

A TERMITE WALKS INTO A BAR and asks, 'Is the bar tender here?'

A PANDA WALKS INTO A BAR, and tells the bartender that he wants to have lunch. The bartender gives him a menu and he orders.

The panda eats his lunch, and when he's finished he gets up to leave. Suddenly, the panda pulls an AK-47 out of his fur, and shoots the bar to pieces. He then heads for the door.

The shocked bartender jumps out from behind the destroyed bar and yells, 'Hey, what do you think you're doing? You ate lunch, shot up my bar, and now you're just going to leave?'

The panda answers calmly, 'I'm a panda.'

The bartender says, 'Yeah, so?'

The panda replies, 'Look it up,' and walks out the door.

The bartender jumps back behind the ruined bar and grabs his encyclopaedia. He looks up 'panda' and sure enough, there is a picture of the panda.

He reads the caption, which says, '*Panda* – a cuddly black-and-white creature. Eats shoots and leaves.'

 A CHICKEN WALKS INTO A BAR. The bartender says, 'We don't serve poultry.'

The chicken replies, 'That's OK, I just want a drink.'

A MAN WALKS INTO A BAR with a duck on his head. The bartender says, 'Can I help you?'

The duck says, 'Yeah, you can get this guy off my butt!'

A GIRAFFE WALKS INTO A BAR. The bartender says, 'Do you want a long neck?'

The giraffe says, 'Do I have a choice?'

A SKUNK WALKS INTO A BAR and says, 'Hey, where did everybody go?'

A MAN WALKS INTO A BAR with a giraffe; they both get a couple of rounds in. When they get up to leave they're extremely drunk and the giraffe passes out and falls over. The man opens the door, about to leave by himself, when the bartender stops him and says, 'Hey! You can't leave that lyin' there!'

The man turns around and slurs, 'Don't be silly, that's not a lion, it's a giraffe!'

A PENGUIN WALKS INTO A BAR. He goes to the counter and asks the bartender, 'Have you seen my brother?'

The bartender thinks for a moment and says, 'Maybe, what does he look like?'

A CROW WALKS INTO A BAR wearing a pearl necklace. He orders a drink. 'I've never seen a crow wearing a pearl necklace before,' says the barkeep.

'What do you expect with basic black?' says the crow.

A PONY WALKS INTO A BAR and coughs, 'Hey, COUGH. Gimme a b—, COUGH, a beer, COUGH.'

The bartender serves him and says, 'What's with your voice?'

The pony says, 'Nothing, I'm just a little hoarse.'

A WHITE HORSE WALKS INTO A BAR and asks for a whisky. The bartender says, 'Hey, we've got a whisky named after you.'

The horse replies, 'What, Eric?'

AN OLD LADY WALKS INTO A BAR with a duck under her arm. A scraggly old drunk staggers over, takes one look, and says, 'Geez, that's the ugliest thing I ever saw!'

The woman turns her nose up at him and says, 'This happens to be a beautiful creature! Go away, you horrid man!'

The old drunk yells, 'Lady, I was talkin' to the duck!'

A MAN WALKS INTO A BAR with his pet monkey. He orders a drink and while he's drinking the monkey jumps around all over the place grabbing some olives off the bar and eating them. Then he grabs some sliced limes and eats them. Then he jumps onto the pool table, grabs one of the billiard balls, sticks it in his mouth, and to everyone's amazement, somehow swallows it whole.

The bartender screams at the man, 'Did you see what your monkey did?'

The man says, 'No, what?'

'He just ate the cue ball off my pool table – whole!'

'Yeah, that doesn't surprise me,' replies the man. 'He eats everything in sight, the little bastard. Sorry. I'll pay for everything.'

The man finishes his drink, pays his bill, pays for the stuff the monkey ate and leaves.

Two weeks later, he's in the bar again, and his pet monkey is with him. He orders a drink and the monkey starts running around the bar again. While the man is finishing his drink, the monkey finds a maraschino cherry on the bar. He grabs it, sticks it up his arse, pulls it out and eats it. The bartender is disgusted. 'Did you see what your monkey did now?' he asks.

'No, what?' replies the man.

'Well, he stuck a maraschino cherry up his arse, pulled it out and ate it!' says the bartender.

'Yeah, that doesn't surprise me,' replies the man. 'He still eats everything in sight but ever since he swallowed that cue ball, he measures everything first.'

A PIG WALKS INTO A BAR and orders 10 drinks. He finishes them up and the bartender says, 'Don't you need to know where the toilet is?'

The pig says, 'No, I'm the one who goes wee, wee, wee all the way home.'

A GRASSHOPPER WALKS INTO A BAR and sits down. The bartender looks at him and says, 'Hey, we've got a drink named after you.'

To which the grasshopper replies, 'What, Kevin?'

A SNAKE SLITHERS INTO A BAR and orders a vodka tonic. The bartender says, 'No, you'll have to be leaving now. We don't serve snakes in this bar.'

The snake is shocked. 'Why ever not?'

The bartender says, 'Because you can't hold your liquor!'

WAGs

A MAN WALKS INTO A BAR, sits down on a bench and orders a cold one. He swigs down the beer, looks in his pocket, cringes and orders another. He gulps down that one, looks in his pocket again, cringes and orders yet another one. This goes on for at least an hour and a half.

Finally the bartender, bursting with curiosity, says, 'I know it's none of my business, mate, but I have to ask. Why the whole "drink, look in pocket, cringe and order another one" routine?'

'Well,' slurred the man, 'there's a picture of my wife in my pocket. When she starts to look good, then it's time for me to go home.'

A MAN AND HIS GIRLFRIEND WALK INTO A BAR and have a few drinks before dinner. The girlfriend wants him to take her somewhere expensive, so he takes her to the petrol station.

A MAN WALKS INTO A BAR and asks the bartender for a drink. Then he asks for another. After a couple more drinks, the bartender gets worried.

'What's the matter?' the bartender asks.

'My wife and I got into a fight,' explains the man. 'And now she isn't talking to me for a whole 31 days.'

The bartender thinks about this for a while. 'But isn't it a good thing that she isn't talking to you?' asks the bartender.

'Yeah, except today is the last day.'

TWO MEN WALK INTO A BAR and start
drinking up a storm.

One drunk says to the other drunk,
'Did you sleep with my wife last night?'

To which the other drunk replies, 'Not a wink.'

A PROFESSOR WALKS INTO A BAR and orders
a double martinus. The bartender says,
'You mean a double martini?'

The professor says, 'If I want more than one
I'll ask for it.'

A MAN WALKS INTO A BAR and orders a drink. After he's been drinking for a while he mentions that his girlfriend is out in the car. The bartender, concerned because it is so cold, goes to check on her. When he looks inside the car, he sees the man's friend, Dave, and his girlfriend kissing one another. The bartender shakes his head and walks back inside.

He tells the drunk that it might be a good idea to check on his girlfriend. The fellow staggers outside to the car, sees his mate and his girlfriend kissing, then walks back into the bar laughing.

'What's so funny?' the bartender asks.

'That stupid Dave!' the fellow chortles. 'He's so drunk, he thinks he's me!'

**AN ENGLISHMAN,
AN IRISHMAN AND A
SCOTSMAN WALK INTO
A BAR**, start drinking, and discuss how stupid
their wives are.

The Englishman says, 'I tell you, my wife is so
stupid. Last week she went to the supermarket
and bought $300 worth of meat because it was
on sale, and we don't even have a fridge to keep
it in.'

The Scotsman agrees that she sounds pretty
thick, but says his wife is thicker. 'Just last
week, she went out and spent $17,000 on a new
car,' he laments, 'and she doesn't even know
how to drive!'

The Irishman nods sagely, and agrees that these two women sound like they both walked through the stupid forest and got hit by every branch. However, he still thinks his wife is dumber. 'Ah, it kills me every time I think of it,' he chuckles. 'My wife left to go on a trip to Greece. I watched her packing her bag, and she must have put about 100 condoms in there and she doesn't even have a penis!'

A MAN AND HIS WIFE WALK INTO A BAR.
The man keeps staring at a drunk woman sitting alone at the next table. His wife asks him, 'Do you know her?'

'Yes,' the man says. 'She's my old girlfriend. I've heard she took to drinking after we split up all those years ago, and she's rarely been sober since.'

'Oh my God!' says the wife. 'Who would have thought a person could go on celebrating for that long?'

THREE MEN WALK INTO A BAR. A drunk comes in, staggers up to them, and points at the bloke in the middle, shouting, 'Your mum's the best sex in town!'

Everyone expects a fight, but the bloke ignores him, so the drunk wanders off.

Ten minutes later, the drunk comes back, points at the same bloke, and says, 'I just did your mum, and it was swee-eet!'

Again the man refuses to take the bait, and the drunk goes back to the far end of the bar.

Ten minutes later, he comes back and announces, 'Your mum liked it!'

Finally the man responds, 'Go home, Dad, you're drunk!'

A CHRONIC DRUNK WALKS INTO A BAR and, after staring for some time at the only woman seated at the bar, walks over to her and kisses her. She jumps up and slaps him silly. He immediately apologises and explains, 'I'm sorry. I thought you were my wife. You look exactly like her.'

'Why, you worthless, insufferable, wretched, no-good drunk!' she screams.

'Funny,' he mutters, 'you even sound exactly like her.'

A MAN WALKS INTO A BAR. 'Give me something tall and cold and filled with gin,' he says.

The drunk on the stool next to him makes a fist and says, 'Hey, don't go talking about my wife like that!'

A DROVER WALKS INTO A BAR. 'What are you up to?' asks the bartender.

'Ahh. I'm takin' a mob of 6000 from Goondiwindi to Gympie.'

'Oh yeah? And what route are you takin'?'

'Ah, prob'ly the missus. After all, she stuck by me durin' the drought.'

AN OLD COUPLE WALKS INTO A BAR, and the husband goes over and starts flirting with some young women. The bartender says to the wife, 'Doesn't it bother you that your husband is always making passes at those girls?'

'No, not really,' the wife says. 'I mean, dogs chase cars, but that doesn't mean they know how to drive.'

A MAN WALKS INTO A BAR. He is so good-looking that a woman enjoying an after-work cocktail with her girlfriends can't take her eyes off him. The man notices and walks up to her, leans over and whispers: 'I'll do anything, absolutely anything, that you want me to do for $20, on one condition.'

Flabbergasted, the woman asks what the condition is.

The man replies, 'You have to tell me what you want me to do in just three words.'

The woman considers his proposition for a moment, then slowly removes a $20 note from her purse, which she presses into the man's hand along with her address. She looks deep into his eyes and slowly and meaningfully says, 'Clean my house.'

A MAN WALKS INTO A BAR looking really moody and immediately orders a double whisky. Then he starts rambling on about how lousy his wife is, until the bartender finally says, 'You know, I don't understand what you're complaining about. All the other guys in here only have good things to say about your wife.'

A MAN AND HIS WIFE WALK INTO A BAR. The wife has been complaining for hours that he never takes her anywhere anymore and eventually he's given in. So they sit down at a table and the husband gets up and goes to get their drinks.

While he is gone a man walks up to the wife and tells her he wants to turn her upside down, fill her with beer and drink her dry. The wife exclaims, 'You sick pervert! Get out of my sight.'

The husband returns and his wife tells him what happened and to go and kick that guy's arse.

The husband says, 'No way, you don't mess with a bloke who can drink that much beer.'

A GROUP OF BLONDES WALK INTO A BAR
chanting '44 days! 44 days!' One of the blondes
is carrying a Cookie Monster jigsaw puzzle in a
frame. The bartender leans towards the blonde
holding the puzzle and asks, 'Why are you
chanting 44 days?'

She puts the puzzle down on the bar and says,
'A lot of people think us blondes are dumb, so
to show them, we bought this puzzle and put it
together. It said 1–3 months but we completed it
in 44 days!'

A MAN WALKS INTO A BAR where loud music is
playing. He spots a pretty girl at the end of the
bar and approaches her.

'Would you like to dance?' he asks her.

'I really don't like this song,' she replies,
'and even if I did I wouldn't dance with you.'

'I don't think you heard me correctly,' says
the man. 'I said you look fat in those pants.'

A MAN WALKS INTO A BAR at the same time every night after dinner. He spends the whole evening there and always arrives home, quite inebriated, at about midnight. He usually has trouble getting his key to fit the keyhole and getting the door open. And every time this happens, his wife goes to the door to let him in. Then she proceeds to yell and scream at him, for constantly coming home in a drunken state. But the man just continues his nightly routine.

One day, the wife is talking to a friend about her husband's behaviour. The friend says, 'Why don't you treat him a little differently when he comes home? Instead of berating him, why don't you welcome him home with a kiss? Then he might change his ways.'

138

The wife thinks that this might be a good idea. That night, the man walks into the bar again, as usual, after dinner. And at about midnight he arrives home in his usual condition. His wife hears him at the door. She quickly opens it and lets him in. Instead of berating him as she has always done, this time she takes his arm and leads him into the living room. She sits him down in an easy chair, puts his feet up on the ottoman and takes his shoes off. Then she gives him a cuddle. After a little while, she says to him, 'It's pretty late, dear. I think we had better go upstairs to bed now, don't you?'

At that, in his inebriated state, her husband replies, 'I guess we might as well. I'll get in trouble when I get home anyway!'

 TWO BLONDES WALK INTO A BAR. You'd think the second one would've ducked.

AN AUSTRALIAN GOES INTO A BAR in the Greek Islands. Jill, the Australian barmaid, takes his order and notices his Australian accent. They get talking and at the end of the night he asks her if she wants to have sex with him. Although Jill is attracted to him she says no. He then offers to pay her $200 for the deed. Jill is travelling the world and because she is short of funds she agrees.

The next night the bloke turns up again and after paying her plenty of attention throughout the night he asks if she will sleep with him again for $200. She figures in for a penny, in for a pound – and it was pretty good the night before – so she agrees. This goes on for five nights. On the sixth night the bloke comes into the bar. But this time he orders a beer and goes and sits in the corner. Jill is disappointed and thinks that maybe she should pay more attention to him. She goes over and sits next to him. She asks him where he is from and he tells her he's from Melbourne.

'So am I,' she says. 'What suburb in Melbourne?'

'Patterson Lakes,' he says.

'That's amazing,' she says. 'So am I – what street?'

'Cameo Street,' he says.

'This is unbelievable!' she says. 'What number?'

He says, 'Number 20.'

Jill is amazed. 'You are not going to believe this,' she says, 'I'm from number 22 – and my parents still live there!'

'I know,' he says. 'Your father gave me $1000 to give to you.'

A MAN WALKS INTO A BAR and has quite a few drinks. As he leaves, late for dinner again, he sees an old bloke begging on the corner. And the bloke says, 'Mister, can you spare a dollar?'

The man thinks about the question for a bit and asks the bloke, 'If I give you a dollar, are you going to use it to buy alcohol?'

'No,' says the bloke.

The man then asks the bloke, 'If I give you a dollar are you going to use it to gamble?'

'No,' says the bloke.

So the man says to the old bloke, 'Do you mind coming home with me so I can show my wife what happens to someone who doesn't drink or gamble?'

AN IRISHMAN HOBBLES INTO A BAR on crutches, with one arm in a cast. 'My God! What happened to you?' the bartender asks.

'I got in a tiff with Riley.'

'Riley? But he's just a wee fellow,' the barkeep says, surprised. 'He must have had something in his hand.'

'That he did,' the man says. 'A shovel it was.'

'Dear lord. Didn't you have anything in your hand?'

'Aye, that I did – Mrs Riley's tit.' Kelly says. 'And a beautiful thing it was, but not much use in a fight.'

HUH?

A DEFINITE INTEGRAL WALKS INTO A BAR and orders 10 shots of whisky. 'You sure about that, buddy?' asks the bartender.

'Yeah, I know my limits.'

AN 18-YEAR-OLD GIRL WALKS INTO A BAR, rips off her clothes and asks, 'Is there anyone here man enough to make a woman of me?'

A man stands up, removes his shirt and says, 'Here, iron this!'

A MAN AND HIS WIFE WALK INTO A BAR. It's their wedding anniversary so they have a few drinks to celebrate a night without the kids. *Who Wants to be a Millionaire* is on the telly above the bar. The man turns to his wife and says, 'Do you want to have sex tonight?'

'No,' she answers.

'Is that your final answer?' the man asks.

'Yes,' she says.

He says, 'Then I'd like to phone a friend.'

THREE MEN WALK INTO A BAR.
Two of the men are talking
about the control they have
over their wives, while the
third remains silent. After a
while, the first two men turn
to the third and ask, 'What
about you? What kind of
control do you have over
your wife?'

The third man turns to the first two and says,
'Well, I'll tell you, just the other day I had her
on her knees.'

The first two men are dumbfounded. 'Wow!
What happened next?' they ask.

The third man takes a healthy swig of his beer,
sighs and mutters, 'Then she started screaming,
"Get out from under the bed and fight like
a man!"'

A LAWYER AND A BLONDE WALK INTO A BAR at the same time. They both order drinks, they are both alone. Eventually, after a few more drinks, the lawyer leans over to her and asks if she would like to play a fun game. The blonde, a bit tipsy, politely declines and turns away.

The lawyer persists and explains that the game is really easy and a lot of fun. He explains, 'I ask you a question, and if you don't know the answer, you pay me $5, and visa-versa.'

Again, she politely declines.

The lawyer, now annoyed, says, 'OK, if you don't know the answer you pay me $5, and if I don't know the answer, I will pay you $50!' figuring that since she's blonde he will easily win the match.

This gets the woman's attention and, figuring that there will be no end to this torment unless she plays, she agrees to the game.

The lawyer asks the first question: 'What's
the distance from the earth to the moon?'
The blonde doesn't say a word, reaches into
her purse, pulls out a $5 note and hands it to the
lawyer.

Now, it's the woman's turn. She asks the lawyer,
'What goes up a hill with three legs, and comes
down with four?'

The lawyer gives her a puzzled look. He takes
out his laptop and searches all his references.
Frustrated, he emails all his co-workers, friends
and clients. All to no avail. After more than an
hour, he reluctantly hands the woman $50. She
politely takes his money and turns away.

The lawyer, who is more than a little miffed,
taps her on the shoulder and asks, 'Well, what *is*
the answer?'

Without a word, the blonde reaches into her
purse, hands the lawyer $5, and walks out.

A BRUNETTE, A BLONDE AND A REDHEAD WALK INTO A FAMOUS BAR. The bartender tells them about a magical mirror in the ladies room. He says, 'If you go up to it and tell it the truth it will grant you a wish, but if you lie – bang! it swallows you up.' The three women head straight for the mirror.

The redhead goes first and says, 'I'm the most beautiful woman on earth.' Bang! – the mirror swallows her up.

The brunette goes up to the mirror and says, 'I'm the sexiest woman on earth.' Bang! – the mirror swallows her up.

Last of all, the blonde goes up the mirror and says, 'I think—' Bang! Gone!

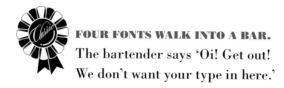 **FOUR FONTS WALK INTO A BAR.** The bartender says 'Oi! Get out! We don't want your type in here.'

MATURE
AUDIENCES
ONLY

A MAN WALKS INTO A BAR and finds a jar full of money on the counter. He asks the bartender what it's for. The bartender replies, 'Every night we have a contest where you have to complete three tasks to win all the money in the jar.'

The man asks, 'What are the tasks?'

'First, you have to go over to Jimmy the bouncer and knock him out with one hit. Then, well, there's a pit bull out back and you have to pull its blunt tooth out. Finally, the boss's wife is upstairs and you have to go pleasure her. But you have to put down $10 to play,' says the bartender.

'Damn,' says the man.

Later that night, after several drinks, the man smacks down $10 and says, 'I'm in.'

He walks over to the bouncer and swings. One hit and he's out cold. The man falls flat on his face too, but gets up and walks out back. The only sound is the dog howling. Then the man steps back in, goes over to the bartender and asks, 'Now where is that lady with the blunt tooth?'

TWO FURNITURE SALESMEN WALK INTO A BAR to commiserate with each other. One says, 'Man! If I don't move some furniture this month, I'm going to lose my arse.'

The second salesman says, 'Watch your mouth! There's a lady sitting next to you. I apologise for my friend, madam.'

The woman looks at him and says, 'That's OK. I'm a hooker. If I don't move some arse this month, I'm going to lose my furniture!'

A MAN WALKS INTO A BAR with a crocodile on a leash. Once he is in the bar he tells all the patrons present that for a round of drinks from everyone in the bar he will insert his penis into the crocodile's mouth and remove it unscathed. The entire bar accepts the dare and each patron puts up a drink. The man walks up to the crocodile, takes his penis out of his pants and puts it into the crocodile's mouth. He then grabs a beer bottle and smashes it over the crocodile's head. The crocodile immediately opens its mouth and the man removes his penis unscathed. The crowd is left in awe.

The man then says, 'If anyone here is willing to do the same, I'll give them $500.'

From the back of the bar a woman stands up and says, 'I'll do it, if you promise not to smash the beer bottle over my head!'

A MAN WALKS INTO A BAR where a fancy dress party is being held, dressed only in his undies. A woman comes up to him and says, 'What are you supposed to be?'

The man says, 'A premature ejaculation.'

'What?' says the woman.

The man says, 'I've just come in my pants.'

HUH?

SIN(X) WALKS INTO A BAR and asks for a drink. The bartender refuses, saying, 'We don't cater for functions.'

A MAN WALKS INTO A BAR and sees a sign that reads:

Cheese Sandwich: $1.50

Chicken Sandwich: $2.50

Hand Job: $10.00

He checks his wallet and beckons to the sexy bartender. 'Are you the one who gives the hand jobs?' he asks.

'Yes,' she purrs. 'I am.'

'Well, wash your frickin' hands,' says the man. 'I want a cheese sandwich!'

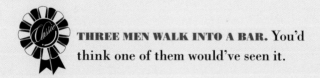

THREE MEN WALK INTO A BAR. You'd think one of them would've seen it.

HUH?

A BAR WALKS INTO A MAN. Oops, wrong frame of reference.

AN OCTOPUS WALKS INTO A BAR and says, 'I can play any musical instrument you like.'

An Englishman gives him a guitar, which the octopus plays better than Jimi Hendrix.

An Irishman gives him a piano, which the octopus plays better than Elton John.

A Scotsman throws him a set of bagpipes. The octopus fumbles about for a couple of minutes without a sound from the bagpipes and the Scotsman asks, 'What's wrong, can ye no play it?'

The octopus says, 'Play it? I'm gonna **** her brains out once I get her pyjamas off.'

A VERY SHORT MAN WALKS INTO A BAR and asks the barman to get him a drink quickly. The barman asks him how his day has been and the short man begins to tell his story.

'Well,' he says, 'I wath driving down thith country road, when I thaw a thine that thaid "horth for thale". I jutht happened to be looking to buy a horth, tho I turned up the driveway to thee about it.'

'The farmer wath quite nithe about thowing me the horth, but I made it clear to him that it had to be a healthy horth, not jutht any old hag back. The farmer told me it wath a 3-year-old mare. When we got to the horth, I athked the farmer to pick me up to thee the hortheth eyth, becauth I wath too thort. The farmer reluctantly picked me up to thee. I checked the hortheth eyth, and they theemed great, and the farmer put me down.

'Nexthd, I athked the farmer to pick me up to thee the hortheth teeth. He wath even more reluctant thith time, but he did it. I grabbed the hortheth lipth, lifted them, and tapped on the teeth to be thure they were tholid. They were, and the farmer put me down.

'We thtepped back thowards the hortheth hind quarter, looking towardth her head, when I athked the farmer to thee the hortheth twat. The farmer grabbed me, picked me up, and thtuck me in the hortheth bum. Then he pulled me out and thtood me up, right at the back thide of the horth.

'Well, I wath in thock. I wath covered in pooh, and thum got in my mouth. Ath I thpat it out, I thaid to the farmer, "Let me rephrathe that. Can I thee her gallop thlowly?"'

HUH?

A MAN WALKS INTO A BAR in Britain and asks for a pint of adenosine triphosphate.

The bartender replies, 'Certainly, sir, that'll be 80p.'

A DISGRUNTLED MAN WALKS INTO A BAR with a stork under one arm and a cat on his shoulder. He says to the bargirl, 'I'll have three pints of Guinness.'

These are poured and paid for and promptly drunk by the three strange customers. Then the stork buys three pints and they all drink them down. Then the man buys three more, mumbling, 'That damn genie!' under his breath as he pays for the round.

Confused, the bargirl says, 'Genie? What do you mean? And why doesn't the cat buy a round?'

'Oh,' replies the man, 'I rubbed a magic lamp and was told I could have anything I desired. Unfortunately I wished for a bird with long legs and a tight pussy.'

A SANDWICH WALKS INTO A BAR and the bartender says, 'Sorry, we don't serve food here.'

HUH?

THOMAS EDISON WALKS INTO A BAR and orders a beer. The bartender says, 'OK, I'll give you a beer, just don't get any ideas.'

 AN AMNESIAC COMES INTO A BAR. 'Do I come here often?' he asks.

BILLY BROWNLESS WALKS OUT OF A BAR.

Hey, it COULD happen!